W9-CAJ-484

DATE			

Cornerstones of Freedom

The Story of
SEWARD'S FOLLY

By Susan Clinton

Illustrated by Keith Neely

CHILDRENS PRESS®
CHICAGO

Library of Congress Cataloging-in-Publication Data

Clinton, Susan.
  The story of Seward's Folly.

  (Cornerstones of freedom)
  Summary: Examines Secretary of State William Seward's
controversial but successful efforts to purchase Alaska
from Russia for the United States in 1867.
  1. Alaska—Annexation to the United States—Juvenile
literature. 2. Seward, William Henry, 1801-1872—
Juvenile literature. [1. Alaska—Annexation to the
United States. 2. Seward, William Henry, 1801-1872]
I. Neely, Keith, 1943-   ill. II. Title. III. Series.
F907.C56   1987   979.8'03   86-30947
ISBN 0-516-04727-2

In 1867, most Americans believed that Alaska was nothing more than a frozen desert. The whole territory belonged to Russia then, and it was called Russian America. Very few Americans had ever set foot there. Hundreds of whaling ships sailed all the way from New England to harpoon whales in the cold, foggy seas around Russian America, but they weren't allowed to anchor in the harbors. The Russian settlers jealously guarded this icy land. They had come there for only one thing—the beautiful brown and silver furs of sea otters. They did not want to share this profitable trade with anyone.

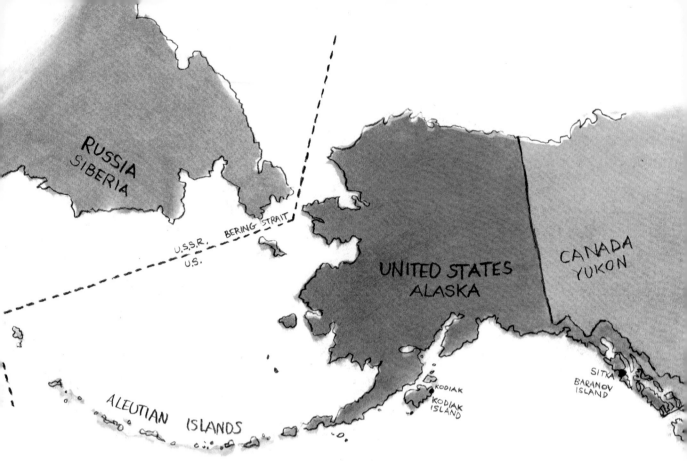

Russia's claim to Alaska and all its otters goes back to the 1700s, when Czar Peter the Great ruled Russia. Czar Peter sent the explorer Vitus Bering to find out whether Asia and North America were joined by land. Sailing east from Siberia in 1728, Bering discovered that a passage of water separated the two continents. That passage is now called the Bering Strait.

On another voyage in 1741, Bering landed on the southern coast of Alaska. As he was heading back toward Siberia, his ship's sails and ropes froze and broke apart. Bering drifted around until his ship wrecked on a little island. Since there were no trees

on this barren, windswept island, Bering and his
men took shelter in the dens of arctic foxes.

Curious sea otters scampered down the snowy
beach for their first look at humans. The playful
otters were easy to catch. At first, the crewmen
killed them for food. But as the winter dragged on,
they began to kill the otters for their rich fur coats.
Bering died on this little island, but some of his men
made it back to Siberia in a boat loaded with
hundreds of otter pelts. When Siberian fur traders
learned how much Chinese merchants were willing
to pay for sea otter pelts, they set out after the furs.

These men didn't hunt the otters themselves. The animals soon became too wary to be caught on land, and hunting them at sea was difficult and dangerous. Instead, they forced natives of Alaska's Aleutian Islands to do the hunting.

The Aleuts paddled out to sea in their light, two-man boats made of sea-lion skins. Then they would encircle a swimming otter and frighten it every time it came up to breathe. Finally, one hunter would spear the winded animal.

The Russian traders had hundreds of thousands of otters killed. One expedition sold over three thousand sea otter pelts for about $150,000. Competition for the furs was so intense that bands of hunters were known to murder and rob each other.

By the late 1790s, the Russians had formed the Russian American Company. Its purpose was to manage the colony and organize the fur trade so that no other nations could barge in. The company made millions of dollars, although it never spent much on settling Russian America.

Fur traders founded the first Russian settlement in Alaska in 1784 at Three Saints Bay on Kodiak Island. Then in 1799 the Russian American Company established the town of Sitka.

Sitka became the territorial capital, but there wasn't much to it. The town had one street leading from the harbor, through a little collection of buildings, and then out of town about a mile toward the mountains. On the waterfront, a battery of cannons protected the harbor. Long yellow buildings with red sheet-iron roofs held pelts ready to ship. Log houses, stores, and offices stood along plank sidewalks. There was a Russian Orthodox church with a green dome and a bell tower. A couple of beached ship hulls, too old to go out to sea, had been turned into stores.

Life in Russian America was harsh. Supplies were often scarce, and entertainment even scarcer. There were never more than a few hundred Russians living in this 586,400-square-mile territory. Clearly, the Russians couldn't keep other countries out forever.

American traders were trespassing to barter with the Indians for furs. American fishermen were eager to try their luck on Alaskan fishing banks. For a time, the Mormon religious group was planning to emigrate to Alaska. For the most part, however, Americans were content to let the Russians have their colony, along with all its polar bears and walruses, rain and ice.

That's why people all over the United States were surprised when they opened their newspapers on April 1, 1867, and read that Secretary of State William Seward had made a treaty to buy Russian America. At first, people didn't know what to think. The *New York Evening Post* called the land a "frozen, sterile, desert region . . . of no value." Then later the same day, the paper praised Alaska's valuable forests and fisheries. One article in the *Chicago Republican* called the purchase "a huge farce," while another article in the very same issue was all for it.

Whether they were for it or against it, newspapers couldn't help making jokes about the new territory. For example, it would need a new name—how about Walrussia? Should we give polar bears the vote? It would be easy to recognize the new congressman—he'd come to Washington "dressed in a grizzly bear-skin overcoat and seal-skin unmentionables."

When people learned that Seward was ready to pay the Russians over $7 million for their cold colony, some of them stopped chuckling. What was Seward thinking of? To some people, the whole treaty seemed like a foolish mistake. "Seward's folly!" they jeered. "Seward's icebox!" But Seward was sure he was doing the right thing for his country. And he was almost sure he could get the rest of the country to agree with him.

William Henry Seward knew that he wasn't popular. Though he had been one of the best-liked politicians in the country, he was now one of the most hated. Seward started as an ambitious lawyer with a strong faith in the United States. He rose steadily from state senator to governor of New York and then U.S. senator. When the Republican party met in 1860 to choose its candidate for president, it looked as if they would pick Seward. But Seward had a bitter enemy in newspaperman Horace Greeley. Greeley used his powerful *New York Tribune* to help squelch Seward's candidacy. Delegates turned away from Seward and voted for the relatively unknown Abraham Lincoln.

When Lincoln was elected president, he named Seward his secretary of state. All through the Civil War, the two worked closely together. The night Lincoln was assassinated by John Wilkes Booth, Booth's partner attacked Seward and attempted to slit his throat. Seward survived, but was marked by a long scar the rest of his life. After he recovered, Seward continued as secretary of state for the unpopular President Andrew Johnson.

Johnson was a Southerner who sided with the North during the Civil War. When the war was over, Johnson wanted to bring the Southern states back into the Union quickly, without interfering too much in their governments. Congress wanted to have more control over the South than that. Seward stood by the president. In the power struggle between the president and Congress, Johnson (and Seward) lost. After that, Congressmen waited for chances to vote against anything the president or his secretary recommended.

In 1867, Seward was sixty-seven years old. One young friend, Henry Adams, described him as "a wise macaw" with "a beaked nose; shaggy eyebrows; unorderly hair and clothes; hoarse voice; offhand manner; free talk, and perpetual cigar."

A politician through and through, Seward knew he would be out of office (along with Johnson) after the election of 1868. He wanted to accomplish something, something important, for himself and for his country before he left.

One afternoon in March 1867, Seward met with the Russian minister, Edouard de Stoeckl, to talk about Russian America. No matter how many times Russia announced that no Americans were allowed in Russian America, it couldn't do much to keep them out. Seward wanted to work out some compromise before this problem caused trouble between the two countries.

What Seward didn't know was that the czar had already decided to sell the whole colony to the United States, on one condition: Russia would not *invite* America to buy the territory—that would be embarrassing. The U.S. had to *offer* to buy it.

When Stoeckl met with Seward, his whole purpose was to maneuver Seward into making an offer. So Stoeckl simply refused to make any compromises. Russia would not let American fishermen fish off the coast. Russia would not let American fur traders into the colony, even if they paid Russia part of their profits. Seward realized that the only choice left was to buy the whole colony. Much to his surprise, Stoeckl announced that the czar was ready to sell.

Seward moved fast. He didn't have the authority to make such a big decision on his own—the president had to agree to it first. Then he needed the cabinet's support. Finally, Congress would have to vote for it. The very next day, the president agreed to the purchase. Then Seward wrote up a treaty to show to the cabinet. The cabinet approved.

In only two weeks, Congress would be adjourning until December. Seward didn't want to give the Senate time to take a stand against his treaty. He also wanted the senators to vote on it before they went home. He and Stoeckl would have to work quickly and secretly. First they had to set a price.

Stoeckl knew that the czar would probably sell Russian America for $5 million, but he also knew the czar would be pleased if Stoeckl could get more. Seward didn't know how much the czar really wanted for the colony, but he couldn't risk the czar's rejecting the treaty. Seward had already offered $5 million, but he had $7 million to spend. When Stoeckl pressed for a higher price, Seward went up to $5.5 million, then $6 million, then $6.5 million. That, he said, was as high as he could go.

Stoeckl objected. The Americans weren't buying just the land. They would be buying all the forts and docks and buildings the Russians had built. The U.S. would have to pay for those, too. Bring the price up to $7 million, he insisted. Both men knew that all the log houses, trading posts, forts, and cannons put together were not worth half a million dollars, but there was no time to stall. Seward agreed. The United States would buy Russian America and all the property on it for $7 million. Done!

Only two weeks after their first meeting, Seward and Stoeckl had worked out a treaty, point by point. Before they went any further, the czar had to agree. On Saturday, March 23, Stoeckl sent a long cable to Czar Alexander. He knew the czar would be surprised. "This whole affair has been managed in the go-ahead way of the Americans," he wrote.

Whether or not he found it peculiar, the czar responded quickly. On Friday, March 29, Stoeckl got a cable back from Russia—the czar said to go ahead and sign. Stoeckl was pleased; he decided to drop in at Seward's house that night and tell him the good news. Now that the czar had agreed, all they had to do was draw up the final copies of the twenty-seven-page treaty.

This would take some time. Clerks would have to draw up one copy in English for the Americans and one copy in French for the Russians. Stoeckl was startled when Seward said, "Why wait until tomorrow, Mr. Stoeckl? Let us make the treaty tonight."

Shortly after midnight, Seward and Stoeckl, with their secretaries and assistants, met again. The Russian wanted a few small changes. Seward resisted them all. To make Stoeckl feel more comfortable about giving up on the czar's last-minute requests, Seward upped the price from $7 million to $7.2 million. Stoeckl was satisfied. They signed the treaty at 4:00 A.M. Saturday morning.

Seward got the signed treaty over to the Senate by 10:00 A.M., two hours before adjournment. Instead of breaking up to go home, the senators decided to stay in Washington until they came to a decision about the treaty.

Reaching an agreement with the czar had been far easier than steering the treaty through Congress would be. First, the treaty had to pass the Senate's Foreign Relations Committee, a group headed by Senator Charles Sumner. Next, two-thirds of the Senate had to vote for it. Finally, the House of Representatives would have to release the $7,200,000.

That Saturday night, Seward set to work on two fronts. He launched a newspaper campaign to win over the American people, and he launched a week of lavish dinner parties to win over individual senators. He immediately released news of the treaty (all but the price) to the newspapers, especially to the *New York Commercial Advertiser*. This paper was run by his friend Thurlow Weed. But as fast as Weed could publish favorable articles, Seward's old enemy Horace Greeley wrote against it.

Weed's headlines boasted "Grand Acquisition of Territory" and "Our Pacific Coast Line Doubled." Meanwhile, Greeley was calling the territory "the

An 1867 cartoon portrays Alaska as a block of ice purchased by President Andrew Johnson and Seward.

national ice-house" and poking fun at Seward's glowing picture of it: "In a comparison of Mr. Seward's documents we find the Polar bear reclining among roses, barley ripening on icebergs, grass of luxuriant growth over which the Esquimaux shuffle with snow-shoes, and Winter everywhere sleeping in the lap of May."

Greeley's wasn't the only voice to speak out against the treaty, but his was the most eloquent and the most consistent. Across the country, many newspapers were against the purchase at first. On April 1, the *New York World* declared, "Russia has sold us a sucked orange." But as newspapermen learned more about the territory, they warmed up to the purchase. After all, it was a tremendous piece of land—bigger than Texas and twice as big as France. The large figure of $7,200,000 boiled down to only two cents an acre! "Dog cheap," proclaimed the *Boston Herald.*

Seward had even more arguments in favor of the treaty. For one thing, the czar of Russia had already approved it. If the U.S. backed out now, it would offend not just Seward, not just President Johnson, but a powerful foreign friend.

Buying Russian America, argued Seward, would also help push the British out of Canada. Of course, it wouldn't be necessary to conquer Canada. Canadians themselves would plainly see how superior the United States was—they would want to join up! After all, what people would want to live under a monarchy when they could govern themselves in a republic?

At this time, too, many Americans believed in the doctrine of "manifest destiny." This was the belief that it was America's destiny to extend itself over the whole continent and even beyond. Seward certainly believed it. He once said, "Our population is destined to roll its resistless waves to the icy barriers of the North, and to encounter Oriental civilization on the shores of the Pacific."

Luckily for Seward, Charles Sumner of the Senate Foreign Relations Committee believed it too. On April 8, Sumner made a three-hour speech advising the Senate to vote for the treaty. One reason was that "the destiny of the republic . . . was to spread over the northern part of the American quarter of the globe."

Sumner's speech was more than an endorsement. Sumner, like most Americans, started out knowing next to nothing about Alaska. In one week he had put together an enormous amount of information, and it all went into his speech. He had temperature readings to prove that winters in Sitka were warmer than winters in Maine. He described the weatherproof parkas of the Aleutian Islanders. Most importantly, he listed all the ways of making money in the new territory.

First of all, trade with the Far East would be easier and cheaper. The Alaskan coast was rich with coal deposits, and American ships could stop there for fuel. Ordinarily, they chugged all the way to the Sandwich Islands (present-day Hawaii) to refuel. Now they could carry less coal and more goods. Besides, the trip to Hong Kong by way of Alaska would be a thousand miles shorter than the Sandwich Islands route.

Fur traders could grow rich selling the pelts of Alaska's seals, bears, foxes, beavers, martens, and even minks. Sumner noted that the mink "by a freak of fashion in our country" was becoming more valu-

able than the beaver. In New York, one mink pelt would bring up to six dollars, but a beaver brought only four dollars.

While no one would want a walrus skin coat, the walruses' ivory tusks were in great demand. In fact, the Russians had been selling twenty thousand walrus tusks a year.

Lamps across the United States still burned whale oil. Much of this oil, as well as the whalebone that went into ladies' corsets, came from Alaskan whales. Alaskan pine trees were tall enough to make masts for sailing ships. Miners could work veins of Alaskan copper and silver and explore for gold.

Sumner listed the fish to be caught: cod, herring, halibut, and salmon. He even included fish stories of a giant halibut weighing 254 pounds, schools of salmon so thick that a canoe couldn't move through them, and whales "so long that people engaged at the opposite end of the fish must halloo very loud to be able to understand each other."

Sumner wound up his speech by suggesting a new name for Russian America—the Indian word *Al-ay-ek-sa*, meaning "great land." People pronounced the word as "Alaska," and the name stuck. So did

Sumner's recommendation. The day after he gave his speech, the Senate approved the treaty by a huge majority: 37 for, 2 against.

The United States still had to pay Russia for its new territory. But Seward had shrewdly set up the treaty so that the U.S. would take over Alaska before paying for it.

On October 18, 1867, Captain Alexis Peshchurov officially handed Alaska over to the U.S. representative, Brigadier General Lovell H. Rousseau. It had taken the two men a month and a half to sail from New York to Sitka. The day they landed, they held the ceremony around the flagstaff in front of the governor's mansion, a two-story yellow brick house.

With Russian troops on one side and Americans on the other, a soldier slowly lowered the Russian flag. While Russian cannons fired a twenty-one-gun salute, the flag got stuck. As the soldier pulled, the flag ripped and wrapped itself tightly around the ninety-foot pole. No one could reach it. Finally the Russians had to lift a soldier up with a pulley. He cut the flag loose and it fluttered down, landing on the Russian bayonets. The embarrassment was too much for Princess Maksutov, the Russian governor's wife. She fainted.

The commissioners made speeches, then Rousseau's son carefully raised the American flag as the cannons started up another twenty-one-gun salute. Three cheers from the civilians, and the transfer was over. Alaska was American territory.

It was a good thing Seward had insisted on taking possession before payment. When the House met in December, they were in no mood to move quickly on the treaty. Alaska did not even come up in the House Committee on Foreign Affairs until March. The czar was expecting his money by April 20, but the committee postponed the bill.

Then all government business came to a halt while the House impeached President Johnson—that is, they put him on trial for illegal use of his power. The effort failed by one vote; Johnson remained in office. But by then, the $7,200,000 was overdue.

The House debate on Alaska finally opened on June 30. It dragged on through the hottest weeks of July. One congressman argued that Alaska was cold, rainy, and worthless. Another answered that "it is not half so barren as members tried to make out; not half so barren as their brains were in arguing against the bill." Finally, on July 14, 1868, the bill passed, 113 to 44.

Stoeckl cabled to Russia, "I cannot give you an idea of the tribulations and disagreements that I have had to bear before the conclusion of this affair. ... Grant me the opportunity to rest for some time in an atmosphere purer than that of Washington." Greeley had his own explanation for the bill's passage: "Only think of a debate on polar ices and polar bears ... with the mercury ranging from 100 to 104 in the shade! Of course, there was no resisting the acquisition. If only for cooling the imagination, it must have seemed dog cheap."

Many of the reasons for buying Alaska evaporated after the purchase. The friendship between Russia and the United States cooled. Canada did not fall away from Great Britain. Whaling, a $90 million business in the 1850s, steadily declined as kerosene replaced whale oil. The fur trade remained profitable, but the supply was not endless. Wholesale slaughter of fur seals brought them close to extinction. Already in 1867, sea otters survived in a very few rugged places. In 1899, it became illegal to kill a sea otter or to sell its pelt.

On the other hand, Alaska had resources that no one knew about in 1867. Sumner reported rumors of gold—someone had once seen a nugget the size of a marble. Thirty years later, prospectors swarmed to the Seward Peninsula, where even the sand on the beaches yielded gold. Alaska became America's forty-ninth state in 1959. Then in 1968 an American company discovered the immense Prudhoe Bay oilfield, holding ten billion barrels of oil. In 1969, oil companies would pay over $900 million for a chance to dig and operate wells there.

Since Seward's day, Alaska has repaid its $7,200,000 purchase price thousands of times over. But back in 1867, one of the senators who had voted against Seward's treaty joked, "I'll go for it with an extra condition that the secretary of state be compelled to live there."

Seward actually did visit Alaska in 1869 after he left public office. To commemorate the occasion, Chief Ebbetts of the Ganaxadi Indians ordered two special totem poles to be carved—one to honor Abraham Lincoln, because he freed American slaves; the other to honor Seward, who made Alaska part of the United States. For the Ganaxadi, the Alaska purchase meant that fiercer tribes could no longer hold them as slaves.

At the top of one fifty-foot pole stood a carved figure of Lincoln, complete with beard, top hat, and frock coat. The totem-pole Lincoln gazed over at the totem-pole Seward, sitting on a box of furs and wearing the tall hat of a chief. Surely when he saw these monuments, Seward must have felt deeply what historians today believe: The Alaska purchase was not Seward's great folly; it was his greatest achievement.

About the Author

Susan Clinton holds a Ph.D. in English and is a part-time teacher of English Literature at Northwestern University in Chicago. Her articles have appeared in such publications as *Consumer's Digest, Family Style Magazine,* and the Chicago *Reader.* In addition, she has contributed biographical and historical articles to *Encyclopaedia Britannica* and *Compton's Encyclopedia,* and has written reader stories and other materials for a number of educational publishers. Her books for Childrens Press include *I Can Be an Architect, The Story of Susan B. Anthony,* and a biography of James Madison. Ms. Clinton lives in Chicago and is the mother of two boys.

About the Artist

Keith Neely attended the School of the Art Institute of Chicago and received a Bachelor of Fine Arts degree with honors from the Art Center College of Design, where he majored in illustration. He has worked as an art director, designer, and illustrator and has taught advertising illustration and advertising design at Biola College in La Mirada, California. Mr. Neely is currently a freelance illustrator whose work has appeared in numerous magazines, books, and advertisements. He lives with his wife and five children in Los Osos, California.